Walther Ziegler

Rawls
in 60 Minutes

AF200872

Translated by
Alexander Reynolds

My thanks go to Rudolf Aichner for his tireless critical editing; Silke Ruthenberg for the fine graphics; Lydia Pointvogl, Eva Amberger, Christiane Hüttner, and Dr. Martin Engler for their excellent work as manuscript readers and sub-editors; Prof. Guntram Knapp, who first inspired me with enthusiasm for philosophy; and Angela Schumitz, who handled in the most professional manner, as chief editorial reader, the production of both the German and the English editions of this series of books.

My special thanks go to my translator

Dr Alexander Reynolds.

Himself a philosopher, he not only translated the original German text into English with great care and precision but also, in passages where this was required in order to ensure clear understanding, supplemented this text with certain formulations adapted specifically to the needs of English-language readers.

For so long as we believe for good reasons that a [...] just political and social order [...] is possible, we can reasonably hope that we, or others, will someday, somewhere achieve it.[1]

Bibliographic Information held by the German National Library: The details of the original German edition of this publication are held by the German National Library as part of the German National Bibliography; detailed bibliographical data can be found online at www.dnb.de.

© 2019 Dr Walther Ziegler
1st Edition December 2019
Jacket design and graphic design for the whole book: Silke Ruthenberg, making use of illustrations by:
Raphael Bräsecke, Creactive – Studio for Advertising, Comics & Illustrations
© JackF - Fotolia.com (image-frames)
© Valerie Potapova - Fotolia.com (image-frames)
© Svetlana Gryankina - Fotolia.com (speech-balloons)

Publisher and Printing:
BoD – Books on Demand, Norderstedt
ISBN 978-3-7504-2784-6

Inhalt

Rawls's Great Discovery

The Harvard professor John Rawls (1921-2002) may well be the most significant of all recent American thinkers. He published his main philosophical work, *A Theory of Justice*, at the age of fifty. Already the book's title has stayed, from its first appearance in 1971 right up to the present day, a provocation for many. This inasmuch as, in the view of most people, justice cannot be the object of a "theory" at all but is rather always a matter of one's personal point of view. Each of us, so it is widely thought, considers, from his or her own perspective, very different things to be "just" or "unjust". And now here comes an American philosophy professor and claims that he has found a definition of justice that is valid for everyone at every time.

Possibly despite, or possibly because of this provocative quality the book quickly came to enjoy enormous success and before the end of the century was known and read all over the world. Today, fifty years later, it belongs among the philosophical classics and counts as one of the most important works of political ethics. There can be no doubt, then, but that *A Theory of Justice* is a groundbreaking work which does not just fascinate politicians and political scientists but has already, in many countries, gained a well-earned place in the education of young people still of school age.

In this important work Rawls poses the great question of the "just society": according to what principles must a modern democracy be organized? Much depends on the answer to this question – including our judgment of the conditions in which we currently live. Because the fact is that we must never be content with anything less than what Rawls calls "a perfectly just society":

> Justice is the first virtue. [...] Laws and institutions, no matter how efficient and well-arranged, must be reformed or abolished if they are unjust.[2]

Already in the very first pages of this his main philosophical work Rawls formulates the ambitious aim of his project and its vast dimensions:

I shall assume [...] that the nature and aims of a perfectly just society is the fundamental part of the theory of justice.[3]

But what is this "perfectly just society" to look like? The question "what is the best possible form of human co-existence?" is one with a long tradition in philosophy. Already in Ancient Greece Plato had sketched out, in his *Republic*, the model of an ideal state that would be governed, absolutely justly, by philosopher-kings thoroughly trained in all the branches of knowledge. Later, during the Renaissance, Thomas More continued this tradition, describing in his novel *Utopia* a thoroughly harmonious society of people living happily together on an island without private property of any kind. This term "utopia" – which More, an enthusiastic scholar of the classical languages, assembled from the Ancient Greek words for "no" and "place" to evoke a "place existing nowhere" – has since become a term for a whole genre of literature and type of political aspiration: visions of an ideal future. And finally, on the eve of the French Revolution, Rousseau, in his *Social Contract*, painted the portrait of a society of absolutely free citizens who governed themselves through popular assemblies.

Rawls, then, was by no means the first to pose this question as to the nature of an ideal, perfectly just society. In the end, however, he provides significantly more than do all his predecessors. In his theory of justice he not only sketches out a utopia – that is to say, a notion of the ideal society as we would wish to see it – but offers, above and beyond this, a procedure which any of us can use to test whether the distribution of goods and opportunities within a specific society is in fact just or not.

Because, as Rawls argues, it is, in the end, not enough to paint, however boldly and imaginatively, the image of an ideal society; one must also be able to make a reasoned argument for why the society in question really is the best possible one for human beings. And here Rawls does something that is very modern: in contrast to Plato and to More he looks, for the proof and guarantee of the notion of justice he develops, to the democratic assent and consensus of all citizens. Only if the principles of justice defined for a society are accepted by all those who have a part in this society, argues Rawls, are these principles truly just.

Basically, what would be needed would be that all the individuals coming together to form a society should agree with one another beforehand, through a contract or "foundation charter" of some sort, about the sorts of principles that should underlie, thenceforth, the social existence they would share. They would need to agree, for example, on whether they preferred a society characterized by class inequalities, such as those between patricians and their slaves or those between capitalist employers and workers, or a classless society without private property, or indeed some other form of social organization altogether:

Men are to decide in advance how they are to regulate their claims against one another and what is to be the foundation charter of their society.[4]

This means that Rawls is an advocate of that tradition in political philosophy that is called "contract theory": a theory whereby a society is legitimate only where all its members have themselves agreed to its laws and basic principles in a contract or founding charter, or where these members can be taken to assent in theory and retrospectively, though born long after their society's foundation, to these laws and principles. In the first of these two cases one speaks of an "historical" contract; in the second one speaks of a "hypothetical" one. According to this "contract theory" of society, then, a society's citizens conclude a contract with one another in which they regulate the fair distribution of all goods and life-opportunities and in which each citizen declares that he or she agrees to abide, in future, by the principles thereby agreed to:

[...] So, a group of persons must decide once and for all what is to count among them as just and unjust.[5]

There really have been at various points in history such "historical contracts" in which a group of people have decided once and for all what was going to count as just and unjust in the society that they were going thenceforth to share with one another. For example, in 1620 the "Pilgrim Fathers", a group of Puritan emigrants from England, made such a contract with one another during the long crossing to America on the ship called the Mayflower. This document, which has become famous as the Mayflower Compact, became the regulating charter for all aspects, both religious and secular, of the life shared by these emigrants in the region in which they later settled as free and equal citizens of a self-governing community.

Being a convinced supporter of the "contract theory" of society, Rawls would surely have wished it to be possible that today's American citizens should once again confer together upon which principles of justice ought to underlie their shared social existence and that these citizens should once again contractually commit themselves to whichever principles they chose. However, even though Rawls was, at the height of his influence as a philosopher, invited to dinner many times by the US President of the day, Bill Clinton, and consequently could boast of having good relations with the most powerful man in

the world, he knew, of course, that no such confer-
ring and contracting together was really feasible. It
also seemed to him illusory to think that it would
somehow be possible to put to the population of the
USA today, when their society has long since taken
the form it has, the question of whether, given the
choice, they would give their assent to, and freely opt
to participate in, the institutions and practices form-
ing this society: namely, the US constitution but also
the capitalist mode of production and the unequal
distribution of goods that comes along with it:

No society can, of course, be a scheme
of cooperation which men enter
voluntarily in a literal sense; each person
finds himself placed at birth in some
particular position in some particular
society and the nature of this position
materially affects his life prospects.[6]

Unlike the Pilgrim Fathers, Rawls points out, we
modern men and women find ourselves born into a
specific already-existing society and are quite simply

never consulted as to whether we find its political form, its economic organization, or the distribution of wealth within it to be fair or unfair. And even if it were to prove possible to consult all those people who happen to have been born in the USA at some particular fixed point in their lives – say, on their eighteenth birthday – and ask them whether they wish to continue to live within that specific political and social order which was contracted into by their country's Founding Fathers or whether they prefer rather to live in some new form of polity or society, this too may not turn out well at all. Because, Rawls goes on, there would always be a temptation for each individual to opt preferentially for whatever ordering of society he thinks will secure him the greatest personal advantage:

For example, if a man knew that he was wealthy, he might find it rational to advance the principle that various taxes for welfare measures be counted unjust; if he knew that he was poor, he would most likely propose the contrary principle.[7]

Rawls, therefore, found himself facing a great challenge. On the one hand he did not want simply to proclaim, as had his forerunners Plato, Thomas More and Rousseau, just his own personal notion of an ideal state but wished rather to go beyond this and to develop a modern, consensual principle of justice to which all citizens of the actual state would in fact assent; on the other hand, however, it seemed to him impossible that any such general assent should ever prove achievable. And even if it should prove so, he doubted that it would lead to a just reorganization of society, since, when consulted as to what they would agree to, citizens would surely decide not on any objective grounds but according to their different views of their own individual advantage.

And it was at this point that Rawls hit on the brilliant idea that was later to make him world-famous: the notion of a "veil of ignorance". How would it be, he asked himself, if, when the citizens were asked to make their choice between the different possible distributions of goods and of life-prospects in the society that they were going to live in, they had no knowledge of their present social position or of the position they would occupy in the society they were going to assent to inhabit? In other words: how would it be if, when making their choice, they had absolutely no idea whether, in the society they were about to establish, they would themselves be rich or poor, male or female, an employer or a worker, a master or a slave, someone with great gifts and talents or someone with none at all? Would they not, under such circumstances, make a much fairer decision about just what the future society ought to be like? This, decided Rawls, had necessarily logically to be the case because, when it is spread out over all,

[...] the veil of ignorance [...] forces each person in the original position to take the good of others into account.[8]

This notion of an "original position" in which people's personal and egotistical interests would retreat for a time behind a "veil" and be completely forgotten so that the people in question, unburdened by self-interest, could look together for just principles on which to build their future society was an idea that drew Rawls so strongly under its spell that he made it the very cornerstone of his theory of justice. He understood, of course, that it is impossible to actually create such an original position and veil of ignorance in the real world because in the case of every real-world political choice the people involved know very well who they are and what it is they want to achieve. But even if the veil of ignorance is only a hypothesis, Rawls proposes that we engage nonetheless in this thought-experiment. He urges us to imagine a group of people in just such an initial situation:

> Since all are similarly situated and no one is able to design principles to favour his particular condition, the principles of justice are the result of a fair agreement or bargain.[9]

And precisely this is the Archimedean point of Rawls's theory of justice and the logical foundation of his entire argument. If human beings were freed of all subjective, egoistic calculations bearing on their own private interest and advantage, then they would come to absolutely objective and fair agreements regarding their future society. Once placed behind the veil of ignorance, argues Rawls, each individual will necessarily strive to find the most just possible solution, paying particular attention to the future fate of the less gifted, less well-earning and less prosperous, since each must reckon with the possibility that, the veil of ignorance once drawn back, he or she may turn out to belong to one of these groups him- or herself.

For example, it is Rawls's contention that, if the choice presented to the individuals in the original position is whether, in the society they are asked to give their assent to, there are to be patrician masters disposing over bond-slaves or feudal lords ruling over serfs bound forever to their lands, or whether the society in question is rather to be one of free and equal citizens protected by a system of social security, the great majority of these individuals choosing from behind a veil of ignorance about their own position and abilities will choose the latter option over the former options. They will do so, says Rawls, because it will only be through this choice that they can be sure that even if, once the veil of ignorance was drawn back, they turn out to be people of little ability occupying the lowest social position, they will still be able to lead an acceptably good life. In other words, the worry that one might possibly be condemned to live out one's existence as a slave or serf will override the tempting prospect of possibly leading a privileged life as a patrician or a feudal lord.

Rawls calls this manner of behaving when faced with a decision – namely, assuming the "worst case scenario" and opting for that particular model of the distribution of goods in which even the least advantaged still gains the maximum possible benefit – a decision complying with the "maximin rule". This rule dictates that one should always prefer, for one's own safety's sake, that one among the various possibilities which assures a relatively good quality of life even to the person at the minimum point on the scale. In the original position, a natural preference for this "maximin rule" automatically ensures that, in the choice of principles of justice by which the society to be established is to be governed, attention will always be paid to the welfare of the least advantaged, so that these people too have a chance of leading a happy and fulfilled life.

In the end, then, Rawls concludes, logic itself dictates that the individuals in the original position, choosing from behind a veil of ignorance which relieves them of all knowledge of their own position and personal qualities, will choose just two basic principles of justice, which he calls the "principle of the equality of rights" and, using a rather more technical term of his own coinage, the "difference principle":

I shall maintain [...] that the persons in the initial situation would choose two [...] principles: the first requires equality in the assignment of basic

rights and duties, while the second holds that social and economic inequalities, for examples inequalities of wealth and authority, are just only if they result in compensating benefits for everyone and in particular for the least advantaged members of society.[10]

The revolutionary nature of Rawls's discovery now becomes clearly recognizable. He answers the question as to what a perfectly just society would look like in the form of a rousing thought-experiment involving three steps:

Step one: He poses the question as to the most just principles on which a society can be based, noting that no individual, not even a philosopher, can establish such principles alone. These principles can only claim validity in the case where all the citizens involved contractually agree to them on the basis of their own free decision.

Step two: Ideally, in order to do this the citizens in question would have to assemble in a sort of "original position" and, choosing from behind a "veil of ignorance" which would deprive them of their knowledge of their own individual positions and thus of their own private advantage, make a fair and objective decision, as equal, free and rational beings, about the best possible principles for this purpose.

Step three: There would result from any choice made under such optimal conditions two, and only two, basic principles of justice: the principle of equality of rights and the "difference principle". These two principles must logically be considered as the best possible ones, since they and they alone arise under ideal conditions of choice.

Rawls admits, indeed, that this choice of equality principle and "difference principle" from behind a "veil of ignorance" is a purely hypothetical scenario which has never occurred in reality and which can in fact never really occur. But he claims nonetheless that the result of the thought-experiment that he proposes is more valuable than all the real attempts of human beings to come to an agreement, through votes or negotiations, on principles of justice for their societies – and this precisely because his, Rawls's, principles of justice have arisen under theoretically optimal conditions of fairness of a sort that no real situation can ever provide:

> It is clear, then, that I want to say that one conception of justice is more reasonable than another, or justifiable with respect to it, if rational persons in the initial situation would choose its principles [...] for the role of justice.[11]

Is Rawls right? Does his sophisticated thought-experiment actually work? Is his combination of equality- and difference-principle really superior to all other concepts of justice? Are – as Rawls's "difference principle" dictates, higher incomes really only justifiable in the case where the financially weaker members of society gain some advantage from the existence of such incomes? Is, in this light, the massive income gap between the richest and the poorest that we currently see in many nations something profoundly unjust? And: might we even extend this rousing thought-experiment of a "veil of ignorance" also to other areas of life? Might we, for example, if we were deprived of the knowledge of whether we would be, in some future society, human beings or animals, then be more inclined to opt for a vegetarian or vegan ordering of this society?

Clearly, Rawls ignites with his theory of justice a whole firework display of groundbreaking new thoughts and ideas.

Rawls's Central Idea

Why We Pose the Question of Justice: The Three Basic Facts of the Human Condition

Justice has been a concern of human beings since the beginning of time. Because every human being, as Rawls points out, has, whether he wishes it or not, an intuitive sense of justice and feels certain things to be "just" and other things to be "unjust". From this Rawls derives three further basic facts about the human race and its condition. He does this by means of a so-called "argumentum a contrario" or "argument from the contrary".

The first fact that can be objectively established about human existence in the world is "scarcity", i.e. scarcity of the goods that satisfy human wants and needs. Such scarcity must exist because – and here Rawls makes his first "argument from the contrary" – if all the things that human beings want and need were available in profusion then the question about how goods can be justly distributed would not need to be posed at all; each of us could simply take as much of anything as he needed or wanted to have. In reality, however, there is no part of the world in which scarcity of goods is not, in one degree or another, an issue. Even in the most prosperous societies the structural wealth is not such that every individual who lives in them can simply consume goods in whatever quantity and quality he takes it into his head to consume. This applies not just to things that are well known to be naturally scarce, such as diamonds, gold or caviar but also to goods we need in our normal daily lives. Thus the supply, for example, of flats and houses close to the centre of the city, attractive training and employment opportunities, and clean drinking water are none of them goods that can simply be increased without limit to keep pace with increasing demand.

The second fact that Rawls see as absolutely basic to the human condition is the fact that human beings are, by their nature, neither completely altruistic nor completely egoistic. This is his second "argumentum a contrario". If human beings were all, without exception, perfect altruists, then here too the question about how goods can be justly distributed would simply never need to be posed, because each individual would be willing in any case to allow many more goods to pass out of his hands into the hands of his fellow man than any system of justice could possibly prescribe that he do. This question of just distribution would likewise become redundant were the very opposite the case and all human beings, without exception, were complete egoists. In this case, these human beings would have no interest in organizing things justly or fairly, because any form of justice or fairness would always be an obstacle to their egotism. Human beings, therefore, Rawls concludes, while being indeed self-interested, also have a sense of justice and a desire to cooperate:

If men's inclination to self-interest makes their vigilance against one another necessary, their public sense of justice makes their secure association together possible.[12]

The third and last basic fact about the human condition is the diversity of life-plans. If all human beings shared the same collective idea of what constitutes "the good life" then, here too, the question about how goods and opportunities are most justly to be distributed would simply become redundant. If, for example, all the members of a society preferred ideally to withdraw into monasteries and to live ascetically and spiritually from the yield of their work in the monastery gardens then they would need no state with laws or rules or any complicated system of just distribution; each individual would then fully understand his fellow citizens' will to live a secluded, solitary life and would respect it. In reality, however, Rawls recognizes, we find ourselves faced with the difficult fact that there are very many different notions of what constitutes "the good life", indeed perhaps as many different notions as there are individual human beings in the world.

The upshot, then, is this: all three of these basic facts about the human condition need to be taken into account when one poses the great question as to what is just. That is to say, one must ask: how are a society's goods and advantages to be justly distributed among its members when, firstly, the goods in question are scarce; secondly, they must be distributed among people who are neither purely altruistic nor purely egoistic but guided, nonetheless, by their own interest and advantage; and thirdly, each one of these members of the society is striving to achieve goods,

and realize conceptions of "the good life", which may
be specific to him- or herself?

For us, the primary subject of justice
is [...] the way in which the major
social institutions [...] determine the
division of advantages from social
cooperation.[13]

Already at this point it can be seen how difficult
Rawls's undertaking actually is. Because the question
of the dividing up among the members of society of
such necessarily scarce goods as income, wealth and
power must necessarily lead, where these members'
life-goals and conceptions of "the good life" are different from one another, to conflicts of interest. People who have little talent, ambition or inclination to
hard work, and whose personal life-goal will therefore most likely be a low-stress, contemplative exist-

ence, will, it may be assumed, favour a system whereby society's goods will be divided absolutely equally among all its members, since in this way they will be able to enjoy a maximum participation in the society's general prosperity while expending very little effort. But people who, on the contrary, possess great energy and many talents or are prepared to expend great effort on improving their lot will perhaps tend to advocate rather a system in which financial reward is strictly commensurate with this effort, so that the distribution of wealth in the society develops more and more toward difference and inequality.

A further factor that must be considered are differences in "conceptions of the good" not just in the sense of different personal life-goals but in the sense of different religious convictions and different fundamental world-views. Puritans who have taken an oath of poverty will likely only consider a society truly "just" if it takes the form of a correspondingly strictly religiously regulated community, Polygamists, on the other hand, will doubtless prefer a society which permits a more libertine lifestyle. But in the end, so Rawls's critics will object, is everything not just a question of perspective? By the middle of the 19th century the consensus at least among English-speaking intellectuals was that "justice" was not something that could ever be the object of objective scientific observation. The influential schools of scientific and philosophical "positivism", in particular, had come to the firm conclusion that the only observations that were really worthy of the name "knowledge" were those acquired through "positive" findings, i.e. findings based on facts perceptible through the senses and verifiable in terms of these latter. In the view of the positivists, opinions relating to matters of good and evil, value and justice related to no such positive facts and were therefore essentially unprovable. In his famous *Tractatus Logico-Philosophicus* the logician Wittgenstein dismissed all supposedly scientific statements about ethics and justice as in reality "nonsense". Ethics, he claimed, was a matter of speculation and thus a purely private affair.

Rawls, however, did not allow himself to be discouraged. He concurred, indeed, that justice is a "private affair" to the extent that each individual will have, at least initially, his or her own private idea of what it is. But if all these private individuals – so ran his simple new idea – could agree upon a single common idea of justice, then this relativism would be overcome.

And such an agreement, Rawls insisted, was indeed quite possible. In order to achieve it one needs only an appropriate way of proceeding. Rawls, then, does not, in the first instance, wish to set up a catalogue of laws for a just society. He is concerned rather, first and foremost, with what he calls "procedural justice". The term may sound rather technical but it refers in fact to something very simple which we often have occasion to use in everyday life. Even little children can be said to apply a kind of "procedural justice" when they are faced, for example, with the problem of how to divide a cake up fairly when several children all want to eat a piece. Obviously, one child will need to be the one who takes the knife and cuts the cake into a number of slices equal to the number of the assembled children. As a general rule, however, the child who cuts the cake will be the last to take his piece:

He will divide the cake equally, since in this way he assures for himself the largest share possible.[14]

Perhaps some such experience during his own childhood even contributed to inspiring the concept of justice that Rawls eventually developed. Because he too proposes that, in order to ensure a just distribution of goods in a future society, there be adopted an ambiguous procedure whereby each person "cutting the cake" does not know, as he cuts it, what kind of rewards will emerge at the end for him.

The Original Position – Zero Hour for the Choice of an Ideal Society

How would a "decision-situation" have, ideally, to look if the individuals in it are to be in a position to arrive at a completely rational and fair decision about the basic structure of their future society? Or, put differently: under what conditions would the choice of such a basic social structure have to be made in order for procedural justice to be guaranteed and the "cake" to be divided up fairly?

Basically, Rawls names six conditions which must apply in this original position if we are to be able to say that an absolutely fair "decision-situation" for the choice of the future principles of justice exists.

1. Equality: All must be able to participate in the decision to the same degree:

> It seems reasonable to suppose that the parties in the original position are equal. That is, all have the same rights in the procedure for choosing principles; each can make proposals [...][15]

2. Sense of Justice: The people in the original position must already possess a certain natural sense of justice and must also be prepared later to stand by the arrangements that they will have assented to:

> Once principles are acknowledged, the parties can depend on one another to conform to them.[16]

3. Rationality: The people in the original position must already have the capacity to make rational decisions. This means that the parties deciding in this initial situation are not complete barbarians but will make use of rational grounds and reasons when they are choosing the basic principles of justice for the state they will later live in. The choosers can, indeed should, says Rawls, defend their own interests in the choices they make; but they should do so rationally and in accordance with a coherent logic, since it is only such a logically coherent defence of one's interests that can possibly lead, in the end, to an agreement on common principles:

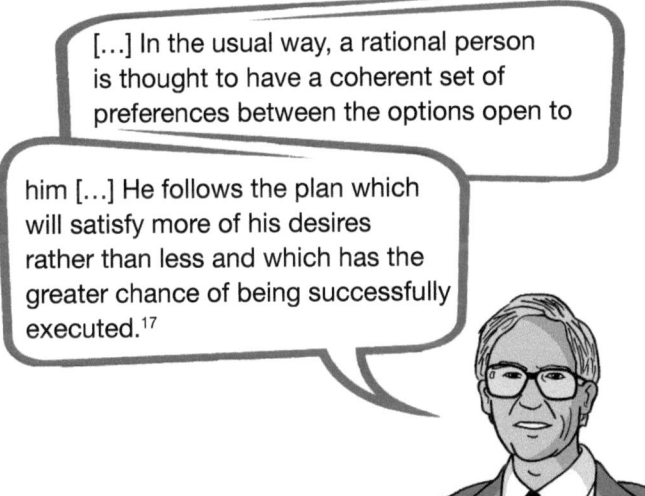

[…] In the usual way, a rational person is thought to have a coherent set of preferences between the options open to him […] He follows the plan which will satisfy more of his desires rather than less and which has the greater chance of being successfully executed.[17]

4. Mutual Disinterest: This condition may at first sight seem a little odd. Why should the people taking part in this choice be without interest in one another? Rawls considers this to be a necessary condition because neither hate, envy, personal dislike or anger on the one hand nor sympathy, affection or love on the other can be at play during the decision to be taken about the structure of the future society, since any of these things could act to distort the result of the decision process. For example, a father who has five sons and no daughter and has been abandoned by an unfaithful wife might be inclined to grant to the male members of the future society a better position as regards reward for work and other privileges, while a man who has, shortly before being asked to choose in the original position, fallen in love with three women might be inclined to cast his choice in favour of the institution of polygamy etc. For reasons of fairness, then, says Rawls, it is best to make it a general condition that the individual parties to the choice have no kind of emotional relation to one another at all. These completely relation-less beings may, indeed, strike us as being not very true to life but, as Rawls points out:

[...] We must keep in mind that the parties in the original position are theoretically defined individuals.[18]

And what is most important for Rawls's purposes is that these theoretically defined individuals should be constituted in such a way that they make absolutely fair decisions. Because it is only thus that an ideal and just society can, in the end, result.

5. *Need for Certain Primary Goods:* The individuals in the original position are not ascetics. That is to say, each of these individuals experiences a need for certain, in Rawls's phrase, "primary goods" and each will prefer to have more rather than less of these:

[...] The chief primary goods at the disposition of society are rights, liberties and opportunities, and income and wealth.[19]

These primary goods have significant importance since it is on the possession of these goods that the realization of any life-plans they may have, and indeed their pursuit of happiness in general, depends:

With more of these goods men can generally be assured of greater success in carrying out their intentions and in advancing their ends, whatever these ends may be.[20]

It is for this reason that it is so important to discover, through the process of decision in the original position, a set of absolutely just principles which will ensure the fair distribution of these "primary goods" via corresponding social institutions. This also applies to one further "primary good" on which Rawls places special emphasis:

A very important primary good is a sense of one's own worth.[21]

6. *The Veil of Ignorance:* In order for no one to be able to tailor the principles of justice that are to govern the future society to fit his or her own personal circumstances and characteristics the parties making their choice in the original position must have no knowledge at all of these circumstances and characteristics:

First of all, no one knows his place in society, his class position or social status. Nor does he know his fortune in the distribution of natural

assets and abilities, his intelligence and strength and the like...The persons in the original position have no information [either] as to which generation they belong to.[22]

Once placed behind Rawls's veil of ignorance, then, the persons deciding in the original position are completely blind regarding their own personal positions in society. They do, however, possess all the various sorts of knowledge about social questions which a rational decision in this position might require:

It is taken for granted [...] that they know the general facts about human society. They know the basis of social organization and the laws of human psychology.[23]

To sum up, then: with the skill of a technical engineer working with pencil and compass, Rawls constructs his original position, out of six component elements, as a "temple to fairness" which draws everyone under its spell. Because there come together in the end, in this ideal initial situation, equal and rational human beings who have no interest in or relation to one another but are rather interested only in the maximization of their own rights, opportunities, freedom, income and sense of their own worth and who, deprived by a "veil of ignorance" of all knowledge of their respective personal circumstances and traits, try to agree on the common principles that will govern their future society.

The Veil of Ignorance and the Maximin Rule

Of the six conditions applying in the original position the one which stands out is surely the veil of ignorance. It plays such a central role because Rawls's most important concern in his theory is to create a completely fair situation, so that the discussion and the choice of principles of justice in the original position are in no way impaired by personal prejudices. And the veil of ignorance achieves precisely this end. It makes impossible, for example, the choice by any of the parties of principles of justice which might go to cement privileges based on race or on some other physical characteristic, since no one, once placed behind this veil of ignorance, knows whether, in the society that these principles will govern, he will himself be young or old, large or small, black or white:

For example, none would urge that special privileges be given to those exactly six feet tall [...]

> Nor would anyone put forward the principle that basic rights should depend on the colour of one's skin [...] No one can tell whether such principles would be to his advantage.[24]

Since the people in the original position, argues Rawls, find themselves in this situation of uncertainty regarding their future positions they will let their decisions be guided by the so-called "maximin rule", namely: "maximize the minimum!"

The maximin rule is a decision-principle drawn from game theory whereby the player, when choosing among several possibilities, strategically opts for that distribution of goods in which even the worst possible result for himself is still better than the worst result in all his possible alternative choices. The "maximin rule", then, involves proceeding on the assumption of the "worst case scenario", aiming to limit one's potential losses, and looking upon the respectively best minimum, among the various social models that one is given to choose, as one's maximal goal. The same wisdom is expressed in the proverb: "A bird in the hand is worth two in the bush":

> The maximin rule tells us to rank alternatives by their worst possible outcomes. We are to adopt the alternative the worst outcome of which is superior to the worst outcomes of the others.[25]

The maximin rule – i.e. the preference for the best possible minimum – thus reflects a rather cautious and pessimistic attitude. In terms of game theory the very opposite of this strategy would be the "maximax rule": i.e. the player, or decision-maker, always runs the maximum risk, that is to say, goes for the option that might possibly bring him the greatest benefits even if this option is significantly more risky.

Rawls, however, proceeds on the assumption that, if people are asked what kind of society they want in future to live in, they will in every case choose that society in which, even in the "worst case scenario", they will still have the assurance of living a fairly good life. For example: if the choice offered were that between a society organized like those of the ancient world, in which rich owners of land and slaves could beat or even kill their slaves whenever they wished, and another, more modern social model whereby, although people would still be dependent on being employed by others, the employers would no longer have any such powers of life and death over their employees, that "maximin principle" which Rawls assumes all choosers will follow dictates that the second model will always be chosen over the first. That is to say, even if the possibility that he might end up living as a powerful landowner with many male and female slaves to do what he will with seems an attractive one to this chooser, he will opt in the end, so Rawls argues, rather for the second, non-slave-owning model, since this alone will ensure him a tolerable existence whatever place he turns out to occupy in it:

It is not worthwhile for him to take a chance for the sake of a further advantage, especially when it may turn out that he loses much that is important to him.[26]

Since, in Rawls's theory, the maximin rule plays a decisive role as regards the later choice of the principles of justice, we will once again illustrate its game-theoretical structure, this time mathematically by means of the following example:

Let us suppose that the individuals in the original position have the choice between three models, each of which foresees goods and life-opportunities being distributed, in the society that they are going to be part of, in a different way. Let the number 1 stand for one gold coin as a symbolic starting capital and thus the minimum quantity of goods and life-chances assigned to an individual and let the number 4000 stand for 4000 gold coins, i.e. the maximum quantity of goods and life-chances so assigned. The question is; which of the following three distribution models would the individuals in the original position collectively choose?

In Model One a portion of these individuals would be assigned only 7 gold coins as starting capital, another portion 32 gold coins, another portion 47 and a fourth and final portion 300. If the parties in the original position choose Model One, then, they know that they will, in the society to be founded, receive either 7, 32, 47 or 300 coins as a starting capital but they do not know which of these four sums will be their particular lot. The same would apply to two other models on offer as possible choices in the original position. The possible alternative distributions would look, altogether, as follows:

Model One: 7, 32, 47, 300
Model Two: 13, 25, 31, 37
Model Three: 5, 417, 1205, 4000

and in all these cases the choosing parties would know that these were the figures at issue but not know which of the four figures would fall to their particular lot.

It is Rawls's contention that the great majority of the choosing parties would opt for that model of goods-distribution in which the smallest possible assignable quantity is greater than the equivalent quantity in the other models: that is to say, logically, Model Two. Because, even if the 13 foreseen in Model Two is no very great quantity of goods and life-chances, it is nonetheless significantly better than the 5 or 7 foreseen by the other two models. It promises nothing like wealth but is certainly the better option in face of the fact that, in the other models, even less could fall to one's lot.

Someone thinking in terms of the philosophical tradition known as Utilitarianism would see things here quite differently. The Latin word utilitas can be translated into English either as "usefulness" or as "advantage" and, from the point of view of achieving the best possible "advantage" for the members of the society to be established through the choice made here, there can be no doubt that Model Three is the one that ought to be chosen. This is because, with its figure for maximum possible assignable goods reaching high into the thousands, it promises by far the greatest potential prosperity and thus by far the best material chances and opportunities for the people who become members of the society that this model governs.

For this reason, several political philosophers of the Utilitarian school did indeed object to Rawls, on publication of his *Theory of Justice*, that his insistence on the maximin principle implied that his preference would go to rather to a society that would be, on balance, poorer than to a society with a higher average level of wealth and prosperity, provided only that the very poorest person in the poorer society were still better off than the very poorest person in a society where people were, on average, much better off.

Rawls, however, refused to accept that such an argument from the "wasting of a chance for a greater collective advantage" was a decisive one to level against his adoption of the maximin principle. The line of moral reasoning developed by Rawls in his *Theory of Justice* is a repudiation, indeed, in its very principle of the typically Anglo-Saxon political philosophy of Utilitarianism, which goes back to the Englishmen Bentham and Mill and the Scotsman Adam Smith. To determine a society's basic principles of justice, Rawls insists, a much greater effort is needed than just arithmetically calculating "the happiness of the greatest number" on a pocket calculator. Such a "utility-maximizing" method, he says, will always mean the callous sacrifice of minorities.

Rawls's way of constructing his "original position" owes, in fact, much more to a moral-philosophical tradition which entered the Anglo-Saxon world from outside it. The persons in this position are distinguished by the fact that, like persons acting according to the "categorical imperative" envisaged by the great German philosopher Kant, they remain constantly aware that the principles of justice that they choose must be "universalizable" – that is to say, they must be accessible to every member of the future society without exception.

Furthermore, Rawls considered his assumption that the people in the original position, behind their veil of ignorance, would choose the option which would secure them even in the worst case a life compatible with basic human dignity to be an assumption impossible to reject already on basic psychological grounds.

The Two Principles of Justice: The Principle of Equality and the "Difference Principle"

All the parties to the original position decide, as equal and rational human beings, how the things that Rawls calls "primary goods" – namely: rights, opportunities, freedoms, income, wealth and the sense of one's own worth – are going to be justly and fairly distributed and organized in their future society. Rawls constructs the decision-situation in such a way that there are offered, as possible options, a whole range of social or goods-distribution systems, from which the parties can freely choose the one which they feel best fits their interests. Rawls discusses, in total, five main solutions to the problem, thus giving fifteen possible choices. In the end, however, the application of the maximin rule from a position behind the veil of ignorance leads inevitably to the parties in this initial situation agreeing to just two important principles of justice, namely the following:

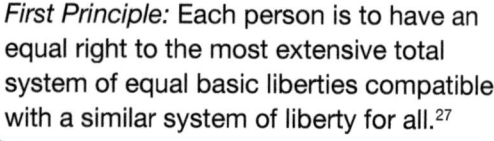

First Principle: Each person is to have an equal right to the most extensive total system of equal basic liberties compatible with a similar system of liberty for all.[27]

Second Principle: Social and economic inequalities are to be arranged so that they are both: (a) to the greatest benefit of the least advantaged [...] and (b)

attached to offices and positions open to all under conditions of fair equality of opportunity.[28]

The first of these principles is the so-called "equality principle". It basically explains and justifies itself. Because, on the basis of the maximin principle, it is clearly in the interest of all the parties in the original position to agree to it that, in the society that they are going to establish, every citizen will have the same basic liberties, since this will ensure that, even in the worst case, none of them will have to accept a lifelong state of disadvantage.

These basic liberties would include, for example: respect for human dignity; protection of one's private sphere; equality before the law etc. No one would wish, in matters of civil and criminal law, to be dependent, as he would be in a society organized in terms of castes or "estates" such as existed in Europe in the Middle Ages, on the arbitrary judgments of courts made up of noble landowners or clergymen. Therefore no one would opt, in the original position, for such a caste society if other alternatives were on offer. Because, choosing from behind the veil of ignorance, each person must reckon with the possibility of he himself turning out to be not a noble landowner or a high clergyman but a serf or a peasant:

Aristocratic and caste societies are unjust because they make [...] contingencies the ascriptive basis for belonging to more or less enclosed [...] social classes.[29]

Everyone wishes to be judged, then, by independent judges who will apply the law equally to all citizens. Likewise, everyone will wish, in contrast to the situation that reigned in earlier times, to enjoy the same rights as others to the expression of his or her personality, as well as protection of his or her private sphere, freedom of speech, freedom of choice of profession, freedom of assembly, freedom of religion, the right to non-infringement of his of her human dignity, and free elections. Thus the necessary choice of the first principle:

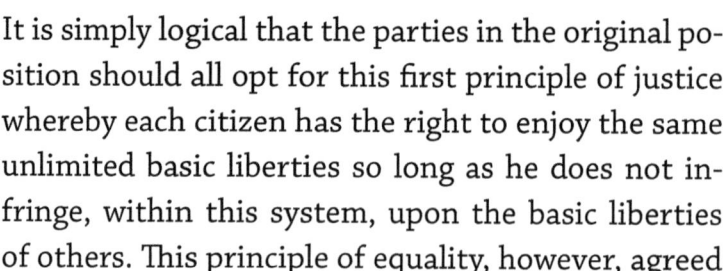

Each person is to have an equal right to the most extensive total system of equal basic liberties compatible with a similar system of liberty for all.[30]

It is simply logical that the parties in the original position should all opt for this first principle of justice whereby each citizen has the right to enjoy the same unlimited basic liberties so long as he does not infringe, within this system, upon the basic liberties of others. This principle of equality, however, agreed to in the original position is, as we know, not only a theoretical construct but has, by our current point in history, become a component part of the political make-up of every liberal constitutional state.

More controversial and thus in many respects more fascinating is the second of the two principles of justice that arise from the choice made in the original position: the so-called "difference principle". Unlike the equality principle, this difference principle is far from being universally firmly embedded in every modern democratic state. For this reason Rawls explains the thinking behind it at some considerable length:

> The second principle applies [...] to the distribution of income and wealth.[31]

And here the result of the agreement reached in the original position – in contrast to that reached regarding the right to liberties – is no longer, surprisingly, characterized by a complete equality:

[...] The distribution of wealth and income need not be equal.[32]

Rawls is of the view that the parties in the original position would opt, in the last analysis, for a differential distribution of wealth and income. These parties, indeed, display a certain tendency to favour equality; in the end, however, a communistic, property-less society in which the means of production and the total national income would belong to all citizens in equal parts, proves not to be the preferred solution. On the basis of their knowledge of the differences in the talents, characters and capabilities of human beings, the people in the original position opt for a correspondingly scaled and graduated distribution of goods and of wealth. This is done with a view to motivating, in ways respectively appropriate for each, all the various individuals making up society, who will surely possess different degrees of talent or different degrees of energy and initiative, and thus rendering these talents, energy and initiative useful for all.

It is an indisputable fact, concedes Rawls, that different individuals bring different degrees of energy and application to their work in society. Many people are highly motivated or are natural hard workers; many others prefer to live more modestly and devote themselves to private rather than professional concerns. Rawls believes, then, that a sense of fairness does indeed dictate that there should be such things as differences in income and consequently differences in wealth and he allows this sense of fairness to come to expression in his theory's second principle of justice. As we have seen, however, this second principle justifying "difference" is qualified in a very significant way:

> Social and economic inequalities are to be arranged so that they are both [...] to the greatest benefit of the least advantaged and [...] attached to offices and positions open to all [...][33]

Just how significant this qualification is is something that we notice only when we compare our current real situation with the ideal society governed by a "difference principle" envisaged by Rawls. We currently see, in most Western societies, differences in wealth and income between rich and poor increasing at an exponential rate, without this resulting in anything even resembling what Rawls stipulates it should result in: namely "the greatest benefit possible accruing thereby to the least advantaged". The huge income and wealth gap opening up between rich and poor, then, is, in terms of Rawls's second principle, a crying injustice:

Injustice, then, is simply inequalities that are not to the benefit of all.[34]

On this schema every entrepreneur, every manager and every especially high earner would need, in the end, to prove that his relatively high salary is justified by the fact that through his performance he helps to improve the quality of the lives of even the least advantaged members of his society. The parties in the original position, choosing from behind the veil of ignorance and following the maximin rule, would, such is Rawls's thinking, proceed upon the possibility that they themselves might belong to the most disadvantaged class in the future society. They would, therefore, prefer in principle an equal distribution of goods. An unequal distribution of goods they would find to be fair and just only in the case where the better position attained by the more prosperous members of society could be shown to lead, indirectly, to a better condition also for all the rest:

[...] Inequalities of wealth and authority are just only if they result in compensating benefits for everyone and in particular for the least advantaged members of society.[35]

Rawls here cites the example of someone who owns and runs a business enterprise. Such a business-owner can and should, according to the "difference principle", earn more than those whom he employs. But, so Rawls's thinking, just this incentive of being able to earn more than others will serve to spur him on to perform especially well in his professional life and this in turn will, in the end, work out:

[...] to the advantage of the [...] man who is worse off, in this case the [...] unskilled worker.[36]

Rawls, then, with his second principle of justice, the so-called "difference principle", comes down very definitely on the side of different degrees or scales of wealth. He places, however, a strict condition on this toleration of differences in income within society:

[...] There is no injustice in the greater benefits earned by a few provided that the situations of persons not so fortunate is thereby improved.[37]

Rawls also speaks at this point of a "principle of compensation" that is built into the "difference principle". That is to say, a just society can and must carry through, by means of its institutions, at least an approach to material equalization of rich and poor, of more and less well advantaged, in order for the primary good of citizens' senses of their own worth to be ensured. Concretely, this means that there must be a minimum standard individual income which will be raised with every rise in the total national income.

But here one might feel entitled to ask: why should that extra degree of performance which is elicited from the more energetic or committed by the higher reward that they are permitted to acquire go to benefit, as is foreseen by the difference principle, the "least well advantaged" above all other members of society? Would it not be much more just if the greater prosperity brought about by the allowing of such a higher-wage incentive were to go to improve the lot of all citizens equally, that is to say, of the middle classes as well as the very worst off? Can we even go so far as to say that the privileging of the least well advantaged that Rawls proposes is itself a form of injustice? Rawls himself, in fact, poses this critical question and answers it with his theory of a "chain-connection":

> Let us suppose that inequalities in expectations are chain-connected; that is, if an advantage has the effect of raising the expectations of the lowest position, it raises the expectations of all positions in between.[38]

If an employer, for example, decides to raise the wages of the "least well advantaged" of his employees, say, his unskilled manual workers, and to pay them as much as he pays his semi-skilled workers, this measure will sooner or later lead, if Rawls's assumption of a "chain-connection" holds true, automatically also to a corresponding rise in the wages even of the better qualified:

> There is no loose-jointedness, so to speak, in the way expectations hang together.[39]

Also interventions by state institutions in favour of the least well advantaged will tend, argues Rawls, to produce beneficial effects for all. For example, where the minimum wage prescribed by law is raised the entire wage-structure of a society will tend to be set, by a kind of chain reaction, in motion. Furthermore, such a rise in the minimum wage will lead to an increase in purchasing power among the members of the least advantaged class, something which will be a spur to the economy and thus benefit, ultimately, also members of all the other classes.

To sum up, then: together, the "principle of compensation" and the "chain-connection" ensure not only some advancement for the least well advantaged but also a higher standard and quality of life for society as a whole. The two great principles of justice, the equality principle and the "difference principle", thus prove to be the best possible principles for securing both basic freedoms and a just distribution of wealth and income. The individuals in the original position would agree, on the basis of their own interests and of observance of the maximin rule, on just these two principles and no others. This is because they would want, on the one hand, in the future society that they are agreeing to live in, to be able to develop and prosper in a manner accordant with the individual gifts and talents that they may turn out to possess but would also, on the other hand, want, should they turn out, in this future society, to lack all special gifts and talents, to be able to take advantage of the "difference principle" and to lead a life concordant with basic human dignity after all. Since, thanks to the principle of compensation, they would never, even if they turned out to count among the very least advantaged, be pushed beyond the margins of society altogether.

Robinson Crusoe, His Man Friday, Scrooge McDuck and John Rawls Stranded on a Desert Island

This contractual model of Rawls's sounds more complicated than it actually is. Rawls's fundamental concern is in fact something very simple. In his theory of justice he develops a clever procedural model with the aid of which each individual, but also a group of individuals, can arrive at agreement on a fair set of principles for governing a societal existence to be shared with one another in the future:

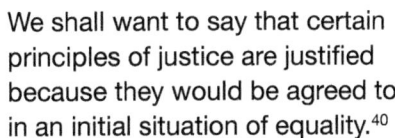

We shall want to say that certain principles of justice are justified because they would be agreed to in an initial situation of equality.[40]

The simplest way to illustrate one final time the model of procedural justice worked out by Rawls is perhaps the following fictional anecdote: John Rawls and Scrooge McDuck wash up, as sole survivors of an aeroplane crash, on a desert island. It happens to be the very island on which Robinson Crusoe and the native of the island whom Robinson has made his "Man Friday" are already living. Robinson orders Friday to take care of the needs of the two new arrivals. Hardly has Rawls recovered from the stress of his hairsbreadth survival than he begins to criticize Crusoe for his instrumentalization of Friday as his servant and for his unilateral arrogation to himself of the master's role. Rawls then proposes that the four of them who now find themselves on the island, discussing with one another as equals to equals, try to come to an agreement about some model of society that will allow them to live there on a basis of fairness.

The others consent to give this a try. Crusoe, however, stipulates that, whatever is decided, he must retain his servant, while the avaricious old millionaire Scrooge McDuck insists that in the island community that they are going to found there absolutely must be a capitalist, i.e. a proprietor of the island, along with a manager and a worker whom this proprietor can exploit. Their discussions go on for a long time. Since they prove unable to agree about who may, or must, take over which role Rawls proposes that the problem be resolved by the drawing of lots. He assigns to the four positions the letters A, B, C and D and fashions little lottery tickets bearing these letters:

A = Proprietor of Island
B = Manager
C = Worker
D = Servant

Crusoe is hesitant about following this procedure and Scrooge McDuck even more so, but he finally comes around. McDuck sets as sole condition that the future society must allow for the possibility of social ascent and of its opposite, so that the person who turns out, in the drawing of lots, to be the least well advantaged will not find himself facing a fate that is unchangeable and, as it were, "written in stone". This condition seems reasonable to all the participants and they agree that social mobility should be an essential component element of the life that they are to lead together, also because this mobility will serve to spur each of them on to perform better in whatever position initially falls to his lot:

Social and economic inequalities are to be arranged so that they are [...] attached to offices and positions open to all under conditions of fair equality of opportunity.[41]

Crusoe, however, insists on knowing, before the decision is made, how much the worker and the servant, respectively, will earn and what they will be expected to do in exchange for these earnings. Scrooge McDuck, an exploiter by temperament, is of the view that the worker and the servant should be given nothing at all in the way of wages: "They should just shut up and work!" "But what will you do," asks Crusoe, "if it's you who draws the lot that makes you the worker or the servant?" "No problem," retorts Scrooge Mc-Duck, "I would very soon have worked my way up out of such a position. I am Scrooge McDuck. I am by nature greedier, and have more business sense and fewer scruples, than anyone else on this island." Crusoe and Man Friday are both unhappy to hear this. "That is unfair," they say. "We might as well just appoint you as proprietor of the island right away."

A quarrel blows up, obliging Rawls to once again intervene. He asks them to consider whether it would not perhaps be more fair and more just if neither Scrooge McDuck nor the others had any idea what talents and character traits they presently possess or will possess in the society to be established – that is to say, whether they are, or will be, ambitious, clever and unscrupulous or rather good-natured, content and easy-going. Rawls explains that he can brew a magic potion which will bring about just this situation: a situation among whose

[...] essential features [...] is that no one knows his place in society, his class position or social status, [...]

his fortune in the distribution of natural assets and abilities, his intelligence, strength and the like.[42]

The others agree to Rawls's proposal and Rawls brews his magic potion, which causes them to forget all their own gifts, special talents and character traits. They each drink their share and it soon works the desired effect. The four are able to discuss objectively and rationally the question of what work the servant and the worker should be expected to perform and what should be the minimum reward that they receive for it if they too are to be able to lead good and self-determined lives. Since each of the four must reckon with the possibility of drawing the lot which will put them in the position of servant or worker, and since, after having drunk the magic potion, none of them any longer know whether or not they possess the innate talents or traits that will allow them to rise from these positions into others, the four do indeed agree on a fair and appropriate reward that will be accorded to the labours of servant and worker and also on the principle that any reward greater than this that may be acquired by the people who come to occupy the positions of island-manager and island-proprietor will be tolerated only on the condition that it works out, indirectly, to the benefit also of servant and worker. Thus, a "veil of ignorance" makes possible, in the end, the unanimous choice of a certain conception of justice:

They are the principles that free and rational persons concerned to further their own interests would accept [...].[43]

To sum up, then: as soon as, on this imaginary island, the individual egoisms of the persons involved cease to be an issue, even personalities as radically different from one another as Scrooge McDuck, Robinson Crusoe, his Man Friday and the philosopher John Rawls prove capable of arriving together at rational and just decisions regarding the future they are to share with one another. The whole problem, then, of the complex clash between subjective self-interest and objective reason that Rawls's system of "procedural justice", expounded over six hundred pages, is intended to solve is summed up in a wryly comical remark made by a German comedian over a hundred years ago: "Man is naturally good; it's only people that are bad." "People", in other words, with their individual peculiarities, points of view and private circumstances, will often, in concrete situations, make very selfish choices and will not feel the need to refrain from doing so simply because others may suffer from these choices; "Man", on the other hand, considered in the abstract, surely does have the rational capacity and the intellectual honesty to make choices and take decisions that are objective and just.

And it is just this capacity that Rawls aims to reveal and recover. He wants to take human beings, who are often, in their concrete, empirical state, "bad people" and transform them, by means of such devices as the original position and its veil of ignorance which strip them of their individual vanities, back into worthy representatives of that "Man" who is, in his essential nature, good. Once placed behind the veil of ignorance, the parties to this original position discuss and debate questions of justice no longer from the perspective of real empirical individuals but rather from the perspective of "Man per se", which is equivalent to the perspective of all human beings at once.

And just this is Rawls's central idea and great discovery:

This way of regarding the principles of justice I [...] call justice as fairness.[44]

In terms of the history of philosophy Rawls succeeds in pulling off, with this discovery, the great tour de force of bringing together two traditions of thought that might otherwise have seemed impossible to reconcile with one another: namely, on the one hand the empirical, Utilitarian approach involving the weighing up of each individuals' personal interest and advantage and on the other the transcendental-philosophical ethics stemming from Immanuel Kant.

In Rawls's model of procedural justice the individuals in the original position are guided in their decisions on the one hand by a Utilitarian concern for their own interests, inasmuch as, by following the maximin rule, they weigh up the likely advantage of any social arrangement against the possible harm that they might suffer from it and opt, through self-interest, to follow the course that minimizes this potential harm. On the other hand, however, precisely by proceeding in this way they also give effect, without, indeed, intending to do so, to that "categorical imperative" which Kant had attempted to argue for on metaphysical or "transcendental" grounds, and which dictates that each individual should act in a manner that is good not just for himself but for all rational human beings and that might, indeed, without contradiction be established as a generally valid basis for all human action. Rawls, of course, is aware of this:

> The notion of the veil of ignorance is implicit, I think, in Kant's ethics.[45]

He admits, then, of his own philosophical labours that:

> The theory that results is highly Kantian in nature (and) I must disclaim any originality for the views I put forward.[46]

It is noble of Rawls to concede that his theory of justice is already comprised in Kant's ethics and that he must "disclaim any originality". He is, however, certainly being too modest in saying this. He did not, indeed, re-invent the categorical imperative. But he did succeed in taking that rule of reason that Kant had been able to derive only from the metaphysical structures of his transcendental philosophy and giving it an empirical psychological plausibility. This he did by creating the scenario of a choice made from behind a veil of ignorance and adding into the mix the maximin rule drawn from game theory. These innovations have breathed new life into the formerly merely abstract idea of the categorical imperative. Rawls, in other words, has pulled off the trick of resolving the contradiction between egoism and the moral obligation to act selflessly for the good of all. He urges us to imagine ourselves as proceeding on the basis of the conditions envisaged in the original position and thus to embrace Kant's ethics of duty – precisely for reasons of self-interest.

Of What Use Is Rawls's Discovery For Us Today?

Improving the Lot of the Least Advantaged – Rawls's Critique of Capitalism

Of what use is Rawls's theory of justice to us? Can we use it to judge, criticize and improve our present-day societies? We have already looked closely at this theory's central idea:

> All social values – liberty and opportunity, income and wealth, and the social bases of self-respect – are to be distributed equally unless an unequal distribution of any, or all, of these values is to everyone's advantage.[47]

Just such a situation, however, is to be encountered today in almost no modern society. Everywhere, we see opposed to Rawls's "difference principle" and "compensation principle" a naked "performance principle".

In a world where the capitalist system no longer has any, or only very few, competitors, the principle of distribution of goods is, globally: "from each according to his ability, to each according to his performance". The upshot of this is that even the most enormous differences in income and in wealth today require no justification beyond the claim that they are the result of the different capacities and performances of different human beings.

In the presently globally dominant social climate, no such compensation for natural disadvantage as Rawls insists on is, in most countries, planned for or foreseen. But just this is a situation that Rawls refuses to tolerate. He contends that, just in the case where a person happens to possess outstanding capacities, he must place these capacities in the service of the community. Because, so argues Rawls, there is no merit in the fact of someone's having been born stronger or more gifted than someone else, just as there is no fault in having been born lacking such advantages:

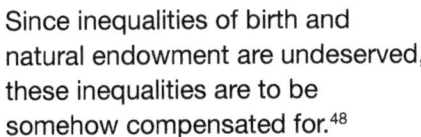

Since inequalities of birth and natural endowment are undeserved, these inequalities are to be somehow compensated for.[48]

It is mere chance or, one might say, a mere arbitrary whim of Nature, that some possess more capacities and opportunities and others less. And this applies not only to the talents one was born with but also to the social class into which one may happen to be born:

Now, those starting out as members of the entrepreneurial class [...] have a better prospect than those who begin in the class of unskilled labourers.[49]

But this advantage arising from birth really ought not to play any role at all because it contradicts the equality of opportunity specified by the first principle of justice:

No one deserves his greater natural capacity nor merits a more favourable starting place in society.[50]

Man, then, must correct with the help of his reason what Nature has done wrong:

The idea is to redress the bias of contingencies in the direction of equality.[51]

Since the distribution of different talents and social positions on the days of individuals' births resembles a mere lottery, human beings have the moral duty to mitigate the injustices arising from this random distribution. The fact of possessing special talents, or of belonging to a financially privileged family and thus of enjoying the better educational opportunities that go along with it, are, Rawls argues, not simply private matters; these talents and opportunities belong, in a sense, to the community and must, therefore, be socialized:

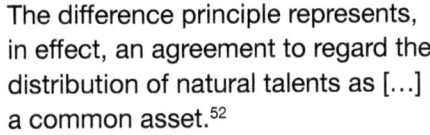

The difference principle represents, in effect, an agreement to regard the distribution of natural talents as [...] a common asset.[52]

Since different talents, levels of education and capacities are "common assets", their fruits must clearly be distributed among all:

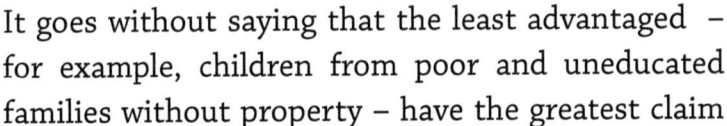

The claims of redress are to be taken into account. It is thought to represent one of the elements in our conception of justice.[53]

It goes without saying that the least advantaged – for example, children from poor and uneducated families without property – have the greatest claim on such "redress". It is particularly imperative that the educational system should, by means of free study-places, grants and other forms of aid, strive to offer, in the long term, the same opportunities for self-development to the underprivileged as it offers to the privileged:

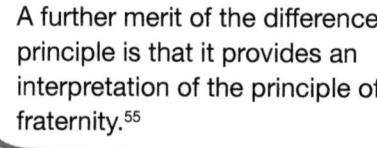

> In pursuit of (the difference principle) greater resources might be spent on the education of the less rather than the more intelligent, at least over a certain time of life [...].[54]

In this connection, Rawls speaks also of "fraternity":

> A further merit of the difference principle is that it provides an interpretation of the principle of fraternity.[55]

Since the French Revolution the three famous demands for social justice have been: "Liberty, equality and fraternity!" The difference principle, and the "compensation principle" levelling rich and poor that is implied in it, correspond, says Rawls, to the ideal of "fraternity". Because among brothers and sisters, as indeed among members of a family generally, it is usual that all earnings, talents and any surplus income are devoted to the wellbeing of those family members most in need of them, or to all members collectively:

> Members of a family commonly do not wish to gain unless they can do so in ways that further the interests of the rest.[56]

Consequently, it seems reasonable to seek this form of "fraternal" compensation and equalization even in the wider social framework. Rawls, indeed, suggests that his two principles of justice give concrete form to all three of the famous rallying cries of the French Revolution:

[...] Liberty corresponds to the first principle, equality to the idea of equality in the first principle together with equality of fair opportunity, and fraternity to the difference principle.[57]

In order to render quite unassailable the equality of rights that he proposes Rawls stipulates that his two principles of justice are to be arranged in what he calls a "serial" order:

These principles are to be arranged in a serial order, with the first principle prior to the second.[58]

This means that the first principle, that of basic equal liberties, always takes precedence over the "difference principle" and that the former can never be infringed or compromised in the name, or for the sake, of the latter. In other words: even if the granting of special rights to some few members of society looks likely to have the effect of massively increasing the prosperity of society as a whole, the equality of all before the law must remain a principle that cannot ever, even for the sake of such material advantage, be suspended or dropped.

To sum up, then: equality before the law is, in any truly fair society, an uninfringeable principle. The only inequality permitted is that in the distribution of income and wealth. But even this latter inequality is limited by the "principle of compensation". There will indeed always be certain de facto natural and social inequalities and these will tend to be reflected in the way goods are distributed in society; but we must constantly be working on reducing these inequalities.

Rawls's "difference principle" and "principle of compensation" amount, at bottom, to a critique of the entire Western world and of this latter's typical mode of production. Because it is a fact that a constantly growing gulf is opening up in the distribution of income and wealth in all those democracies whose economies are based on free-market principles. We see more and more extreme examples of gaps between the incomes of the rich and the poor that would be impossible to justify on the terms that Rawls sets for a fair society. Thus, already at the time of the fall of the Berlin Wall the members of the boards of the 30 top companies quoted on the Frankfurt Stock Exchange were earning, on average, fourteen times what these companies' typical employees were earning. Today, thirty years later, a study by the Hans Böckler Institute [59] shows that these board members earn between sixty and a hundred times as much as their employees:

A scheme is unjust when the higher expectations [...] are excessive.[60]

In 2018 Bob Iger, the CEO and Chairman of the Walt Disney company, was receiving a total annual remuneration of over 146 million dollars, some five hundred times the salary received by the average Disney employee. Tim Cook, the CEO of Apple, received a comparably fabulous total remuneration that year, 141 million dollars, which doubtless stands in a similar ratio to the salary of the average Apple employee.

According to Rawls's "principle of compensation" such huge disproportions between the salaries of senior management would only be justifiable if it could be proven, firstly, that Messrs. Iger and Cook did their work five hundred times more effectively than did the average employee of their companies and, secondly, that these extraordinary work-performances of the two top managers had gone to massively improve the condition of the least advantaged employees within these companies and massively helped these latter to progress. Should this not be the case, such huge disproportions in remuneration would, for Rawls, represent clear instances of "injustice":

Injustice, then, is simply inequalities that are not to the benefit of all.[61]

Likewise "unjust", by this standard, would be the drastic rises in rents currently going on in many of the world's great cities, the real estate market having been overheated by the growing shortage of living space. Because such rent rises are leading to record increases in the profits of property-owners without the tenants having any part or share in this. In order to meet the moral standard set by Rawls's "difference principle" large property magnates would need to demonstrably re-invest their profits in the modernization of their properties or in the construction of new buildings, so that there would eventually come to be sufficient, and qualitatively satisfactory, housing available even for the least advantaged. Such constructive re-investment, however, is far from being the rule and, even where it is claimed to have occurred, is difficult to prove. Despite the extreme difficulty of proving, however, whether or not earnings and wealth have, in any particular case, really been channelled back to the benefit of the less advantaged, Rawls insists that his theory of justice does indeed contain an objective standard and measure:

The difference principle tries to establish objective grounds for interpersonal comparisons [...].[62]

But just where does the objective limit lie? Beyond what point are inequalities in income and wealth "unjust"? And below what point must a citizen count as one of the "least advantaged" who is entitled to help from society as a whole? Does there really exist a practically applicable measure to establish what a "fair" distribution of goods and resources through our social institutions would be – or is Rawls's notion of "distributive justice" in the end nothing but an impractical theory?

Fair Distribution of Goods and Resources: Realizable in Practice or Pure Theory?

As a response to the charge that his model of justice is "pure theory" without possible practical application Rawls proposes that there be applied, as a means of identifying "the least advantaged", the concrete standard: "half of the median": whoever, in any particular state, earns less than half of the average income in said state, must count as one of these "least advantaged" and shall have a right to aid and support from the commonweal as soon as the better-earning citizens of the same state are able to increase their own income:

> [...] There is no injustice in the greater benefits earned by a few provided that the situation of persons not so fortunate is thereby improved.[63]

Certain questions, however, still remain unanswered. Just how much more than the average are these "few" permitted to earn? How exactly is it to be established whether, say, a businessman's investment in some new technology is something likely to "benefit all" or not? Is the million-dollar salary of a professional athlete justified by the fact alone that "the least advantaged" can take delight in watching him play football or basketball with consummate skill, or would there have to be proven here, in order for such a salary to be just, that it somehow brings about a real transfer of wealth to the poor?

The question of how the "principle of compensation" is to be concretely applied is, without any doubt, a difficult one. It must, however, be recognized that Rawls stands out as an exception among social and political theorists today by reason of his having refused the predominant approach of justifying income, however exorbitant, purely by reference to the play of supply and demand and his having opposed to this a very different model of justification. Whereas, before Rawls, the super-rich and super-high-earners, when challenged about the exorbitant rewards they were reaping, felt they needed to say no more than "it's what the market dictates", Rawls's theory of justice has called "the market" into question as a valid court of moral appeal. His work has reminded us that it is indeed entirely possible to set limits to how high individual salaries can rise, regardless of "what the market dictates", and to carry out a redistribution of wealth from rich to poor through the system of taxation:

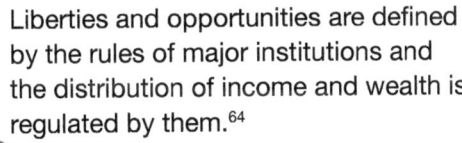

Liberties and opportunities are defined by the rules of major institutions and the distribution of income and wealth is regulated by them.[64]

By putting in this way his "procedural justice" in the place of the supposed "justice of the market" Rawls contravened a central taboo of economic liberalism.

He dared to cast doubt on the sacredness of the market and its supposed powers of self-regulation and proposed, backing up his proposal with reasons and arguments, that there be adopted in its stead a way of regulating social problems inspired by a concern for justice alone. It may well have been for this reason that *A Theory of Justice* went on to be translated into two dozen languages and became, within a few short years, a work well known all over the globe.[65]

Rawls's masterpiece, however, also attracted, as is the case with every great theory, much criticism. It has been objected, for example, to the model developed by Rawls that that hypothetical choice in an "original position" which he envisages is not, in fact, so designed that it provides a genuinely democratic justification for Rawls's two principles of justice. This is the case, so it has been argued, insofar as, on closer examination, the "original position" itself proves deeply undemocratic. Real democracies, so Rawls's critics have objected, are "pluralistic" in the strongest possible sense of this term; in such societies, different individuals and parties with different views and interests discuss and debate until they arrive at compromise positions that can pass for just solutions. But the very nature of the "original position" as Rawls designs and sketches it is such that no such discussions or debates can really occur there. This, say his critics, is because Rawls has woven his "veil of ignorance" far too thick: his overriding concern with constructing the parties to the decision in the "original position" as individuals who must be recognized as fair, objective and absolutely unpartisan has had the result that these parties are not, in the end, really individuals at all and the groups that they represent are not really groups with concrete interests such as exist in real life.

In other words: once Rawls has made human beings fit to participate in the choice of principles of justice under supposedly "ideal conditions", what is left are not human beings but only sterile, relation-less and emotion-less clones who no longer know even who they are or who they will be. This being the case, how can we really speak of such beings choosing principles of justice "such as will serve their own interests"? Rawls describes, indeed, the "original position" as if it were a matter of a diverse and plural group of human beings coming together to arrive at a fair agreement; really, though, given the "clone-like" nature of the parties behind the thick, de-individualizing "veil of ignorance", it would be more accurate to speak of the decision on the principles of justice being made here by a single, artificial "macro-subject".[66]

Other critics have raised the following objection: Rawls himself stipulates that the parties in the "original position" must possess, in order to make a good decision, a well-founded basic knowledge of the principles of politics, economics and human psychology; but Rawls's hypothetical situation is constructed in such a way that it would be impossible for the parties in question to have such knowledge since, deciding from behind so "thick" a "veil of ignorance", they are deprived of all that personal experience of economic advantage or non-advantage from which such well-founded knowledge could alone arise.

Criticisms have also been made of the maximin rule. Human beings, it has been objected, are nowhere near so averse to taking risks as Rawls supposes them to be: where there is a prospect of acquiring great advantages they may, under certain circumstances, disregard the possible negative effects of their decisions. Thus, instead of making a pessimistic "worst-case scenario" mentality the key psychological trait of the parties in his "original position", Rawls ought rather, so runs this objection, to have assumed, for these parties, an average readiness to run risks in the hope of rewards.[67]

There may be some truth to these various criticisms that have been raised of the theoretical coherence of

Rawls's "original position". One may nevertheless be surprised at the fact that this "original position" and the "veil of ignorance" that defines it have been the object of such a rigorous critical examination, and even of outright rejection, by so many contemporary thinkers. Because one thing is for certain: in his way of designing the "original position" Rawls was really only taking up an ancient image typical of and central to our culture which is well known to us all and quite inseparable from our commonly-held notion of justice: namely, the image of the goddess Justicia, with her famous sword and scales and the even more famous blindfold over her eyes.

For thousands of years already the goddess of justice has been portrayed with these three key attributes. The scales stand for the law, whereby she carefully weighs right and wrong against one another; the sword for the punishment that she visits upon any contravention of this law; and the blindfold for the absolutely unpartisan stance she adopts between any two parties seeking justice. Because Justicia, as the saying goes, is "no respecter of persons" and will pass her judgment on the basis of the facts alone regardless of how personally pleasing or unpleasing the parties coming before her may be. She shows sympathy neither for the accuser nor for the accused. Her gaze is directed exclusively inwardly, toward the pure Idea of Justice. And it is to this idea and this idea alone that Rawls attempts to give expression through his "original position": non-partisanship in its fully and consistently developed form.

The Veil of Ignorance: A Principle of Decision That Can Also Be Applied in Other Fields?

Some years after the publication of his major work Rawls transposed his highly engaging thought experiment of a "veil of ignorance" also into the field of international law and international relations. Once again he imagines a fictive "original position" and poses the question: what kind of contract or convention governing international relations would emerge if the different nations – or, as he prefers to say, "peoples" – of the globe were able to decide on one under the best possible conditions?

Let us suppose that the representatives of these peoples of the globe met together and consulted with one another, under a "veil of ignorance" of the kind that we have discussed, about what sort of international legal order ought to reign. In this case the "veil of ignorance" would bring it about that the parties to the consultation would know neither the size nor the military strength of the particular nation that each of them represented:

More than this, I assume that the parties do not know the particular circumstances of their own

society. That is, they do not know its economic or political situation or the level of civilization and culture it has been able to achieve.[68]

The parties will each be quite unaware, then, of whether the nation they represent is a poor developing country or a leading industrial nation. What kind of future "world order" would they choose, choosing from behind such a "veil of ignorance"? Rawls assumes that the upshot of such a choice made from behind a "veil of ignorance" would be a world order in which all states, regardless of their respective sizes and degrees of power, would respect each other as free and equal partners. More specifically, they would, Rawls argues, opt for the following basic principles which, it might be noted in passing, coincide very closely with the actual guiding principles of today's real international law:

Peoples are free and independent [...] (and) are to observe treaties and undertakings [...]

Peoples are equal and are parties to the agreements that bind them [...] Peoples are to observe a duty of non-intervention [...] Peoples have the right of self-defence [...] Peoples are to honour human rights.[69]

What is more, and on this point Rawls lays particular weight:

Peoples have a duty to assist other peoples living under unfavourable conditions.[70]

Commenting on how this final principle, a duty of assistance, might be given concrete form, Rawls adds that, in any Law of Peoples:

> Certain provisions will be included for mutual assistance among peoples in times of famine and drought [...].[71]

The result emerging from Rawls's book *The Law of Peoples*, then, matches that which emerged from *A Theory of Justice*, with the sole difference that the principles of justice chosen apply no longer to the co-existence of individuals within a single society but, now, to the co-existence of entire nations on the level of the planet as a whole.

In both cases, however, it is agreed, from behind a "veil of ignorance", that the parties shall in future treat each other fairly and as equal partners in a common undertaking and also that there should exist a common duty to come to the aid of the least advantaged. Rawls, furthermore, himself stresses that his thought experiment can be carried over not just into the field of international law but into other fields as well:

In any case, the original position must be interpreted so that one can at any time adopt its perspective.[72]

This "original position behind the veil of ignorance" is in the last analysis, as Rawls himself states, no "ideal" that lies beyond our power to attain. On the contrary, any one of us can, even in the midst of his or her everyday life, step into this "original position" and apply the "veil of ignorance" as a practical procedure. One needs only to imagine, for just a moment, this notion of a "veil":

At any time we can enter the original position, so to speak, simply by following a certain procedure: namely, by arguing for principles of justice in accordance with these restrictions.[73]

For example, were a discussion and debate to be begun about setting a legal minimum wage for barbers, many people might, at the start, be against such a proposal, fearing (perhaps rightly) that a visit to the barber shop might become much more expensive as a result. But if we, as Rawls recommends, place ourselves mentally for a moment "behind the veil of ignorance" and imagine that we no longer know whether we ourselves will be, in some future society, a barber or one of his customers, we thereby automatically, by imaginatively imposing this restriction on our own knowledge, project ourselves much more intensively than we would otherwise have been able to do into the situation of the underpaid barbers. This means, in turn, that we decide the question much more justly. And just this is the effect of Rawls's thought-experiment:

One excludes the knowledge of those contingencies which [...] allows (men) to be guided by their prejudices.[74]

Rawls formulates this idea even more clearly when he says that his thought-experiment of the "veil of ignorance":

[...] forces each person [...] to take the good of others into account.[75]

One might find a further possible application for Rawls's thought-experiment in political veganism, with regard specifically to the legitimation of the notion of animal rights. Here too one might proceed from a hypothetical "original position". Let us imagine that all the living beings that might possibly be affected by this issue were asked to make a decision "from behind the veil of ignorance" – i.e. in a state of radical uncertainty about whether they were in future to be human beings or non-human animals – regarding the principles of justice that would henceforth govern society. They would have to choose between four possibilities:

Firstly, a "cannibalistic society" in which all would be permitted to kill and eat anyone or anything, be it animal or human being.

Secondly, a "carnivorous society" in which it would be permitted to kill and eat non-human animals but not human beings.

Thirdly, a "vegetarian society" in which it would not be permitted to kill or eat either humans or non-human animals but in which the freedom and the bodily integrity of these latter would, nonetheless, be severely compromised, with cows, for example, being kept in stalls so as to have their milk industrially extracted from them.

Fourthly, a "vegan society" in which the absolute right to life and to liberty would be guaranteed equally both to humans and to all non-human animals.

If we assume, as Rawls does, a choice according to the "maximin principle", we must suppose that the majority of those choosing would opt for the principle of justice represented by the vegan society, so as to exclude completely the possibility that they themselves might be eaten or, failing that, locked away and forcibly milked. And there are surely many other such possible examples, i.e. possible ways of applying Rawls's basic concept so as to shake up accustomed habits of thought and draw new potential principles of justice into the realm of public discourse:

We should view a theory of justice as a guiding framework designed to focus our moral sensibilities [...].[76]

Rawls's Legacy: The Undying Demand for Justice

Rawls received great recognition for his theory of justice but it also prompted a veritable avalanche of critical reactions. Philosophers belonging to the Utilitarian tradition find fault, still today, with Rawls's theory for placing, due to its following of the "maximin rule", the welfare of the least advantaged above that of the community as a whole; socialists and communists consider the theory's "difference principle", which permits differences of income and wealth in the society chosen by the parties to the "original position", to be a betrayal of the principle of the equality of all human beings; while thinkers of neo-liberal persuasion, quite to the contrary, see in this "difference principle" an unjustifiable levelling-down of individuals distinct in talent and merit. Rawls's theory of justice, then, has been the target of attacks coming from all across the political spectrum: from socialists who look on the theory as legitimizing an inegalitarianism almost as callous as that of neo-liberalism to neo-liberals who look on it as a barely disguised form of socialism.

One can indeed legitimately subscribe to any one of a whole range of evaluations of Rawls's theory. One thing, however, is undeniable: in contrast to Plato and many others, Rawls not only formulated the vision of a just society but also provided modern, democratic reasons and foundations for this vision.

Because, Rawls insists, every being endowed with reason can and will concur with the two basic principles of justice that he proposes, provided only that his theory does indeed effectively prove that these principles are those which would have arisen in the "original position", under absolutely fair and appropriate conditions, and can be logically derived from this latter:

The original position is, one might say, the appropriate initial status quo, and thus the fundamental agreements reached in it are fair.[77]

At this point many of Rawls's critics raised the following objection: it may indeed be the case that the two principles can be logically derived from a completely fair agreement carried through in such an "original position". But such an agreement made "from behind a veil of ignorance" has in fact never really taken place and is so constituted that it can never really take place even at some point in the future.[78] Rawls, however, was himself aware of this problem. Indeed, he envisages the posing of just this question:

It is natural to ask why, if this agreement is never actually entered into, we should take any interest in these principles [...].[79]

But he also has a response to this question:

The answer is that the conditions embodied in the description of the original position are ones that we do in fact accept.[80]

His argument here is the following one: if we, i.e. his readers, come in the end to accept the original position and those conditions, that he so carefully thought out, underlying it, then it is a matter of no importance whether such things ever really existed or not, because we legitimate the original position retroactively through our democratic assent to it. The most ingenious thing about Rawls's theoretical construction is that he obliges each of us, in the end, to come to some clarity about whether we can assent to his conception or not, for just this forms the core of his consensually democratic demonstration of the truth of his theory. Rawls, of course, would like that we give this assent; but his tone remains, nonetheless, as behoves a philosopher, a modest and tentative one:

I do not expect the answer I [...] suggest to be convincing to everyone.[81]

One can, then, be either in agreement or in disagreement with the fair conditions in the "original position" and with the principles of justice emerging from it. In either case, however, Rawls compels us to take a stance. He places us adamantly and unrelentingly before the demand that we give our own personal answer to the question of what is just or unjust, fair or unfair.

His worldwide fame is essentially connected with the fact that, for all the modest and soberly rational style of his philosophy, he has nonetheless become one of the great provocateurs of present-day political theory. He provokes us, specifically, into deciding for ourselves what is just and unjust, rather than continuing to leave the task of defining "justice" in the hands of the state, of politicians and of jurists.

With his "veil of ignorance" he has provided us with

a rich and fascinating decisional procedure by means of which we can review and validate, in every situation and at any time, our own ideas about justice. We find ourselves indeed, as inhabitants of the modern world, born always into the midst of conventions, legal systems and other constraints on our action which we had, in fact, no personal part in choosing. But this is no reason, Rawls tells us, to look on these things as eternally unalterable and as having to be accepted for what they are:

[...] We can still ask what a perfectly just society would be like.[82]

Bibliographical References

1   John Rawls, The Law of Peoples, Harvard University Press, Cambridge Massachusetts, 1999, p. 128
2   John Rawls, A Theory of Justice (Revised Edition), Oxford University Press 1999, p. 3.
3   Ibid. p. 8.
4   Ibid. p. 10.
5   Ibid. p. 11.
6   Ibid. p. 12.
7   Ibid. p. 17.
8   Ibid. pp. 128-129.
9   Ibid. p. 11
10   Ibid. p. 13
11   Ibid. pp. 15-16.
12   Ibid. pp. 4-5.
13   Ibid. p. 6.
14   Ibid. p. 74.
15   Ibid. p. 17.
16   Ibid. p. 125.
17   Ibid. p. 124.
18   Ibid. p. 127.
19   Ibid. p. 54.
20   Ibid. p. 79.
21   Ibid.
22   Ibid. p. 118.
23   Ibid. p. 119.
24   Ibid. p. 129.
25   Ibid. p. 133.
26   Ibid. p. 134.
27   Ibid. p. 266.
28   Ibid.
29   Ibid. p. 87-88.
30   Ibid. p. 266.
31   Ibid. p. 53.
32   Ibid.
33   Ibid. p. 266.

34 Ibid. p. 54.
35 Ibid. p. 13.
36 Ibid. p. 68.
37 Ibid. p. 13.
38 Ibid. p. 69.
39 Ibid. p. 70.
40 Ibid. p. 19.
41 Ibid. p. 266.
42 Ibid. p. 11.
43 Ibid. p. 10.
44 Ibid.
45 Ibid. p. 121
46 Ibid. p. xviii (Preface)
47 Ibid. p. 54.
48 Ibid. p. 86.
49 Ibid. p. 67.
50 Ibid. p. 87.
51 Ibid. p. 86.
52 Ibid. p. 87.
53 Ibid. p. 86.
54 Ibid.
55 Ibid. p. 90.
56 Ibid.
57 Ibid. p. 91.
58 Ibid. p. 53.
59 See Marion Weckes, Manager to Worker Pay Ratio 2017, published by the Institut für Mitbestimmung und Unternehmensführung of the Hans Böckler Institute: "The present study analyses the manager-to-worker pay ratio for every enterprise appearing on the Dax 30. It shows the gap between the remuneration received by the management boards of these enterprises (both as a whole and specifying the salaries of the CEO and the board members individually) and that received by the employees [...] The results indicate that this gap is rapidly growing. Whereas the ratio between managers' and workers' pay lay, in the companies that made up the Dax 30 in 2005, somewhere around 42 to 1, by 2011 it stood at 62 to 1. By 2017 it was on average 71 to 1."
60 John Rawls, A Theory of Justice (Revised Edition), Oxford University Press 1999, p. 68.

61 Ibid. p. 54.

62 Ibid. p. 79.

63 Ibid. p. 13.

64 Ibid. p. 79.

65 For over twenty years A Theory of Justice, published in 1971, sufficed in itself to ensure worldwide fame for Rawls and his ideas. It was only in 1993 that he brought out a second book, likewise a substantial volume, entitled Political Liberalism. Naturally, this second book has never attained to the status of being almost a "household name" that the work of 1971 did. It adds, however, certain important nuances and changes of emphasis to the first great work. In particular, it responds to the criticisms levelled against A Theory of Justice that the parties choosing in Rawls's "original position" did not really reflect the citizens of our increasingly "pluralist" societies with their radically different and conflicting "conceptions of 'the good'". See John Rawls, Political Liberalism, Columbia University Press, New York, 1993.

66 These critical reactions to Rawls's book of 1971 that gradually accumulated in the ten years after its publication meant that political-philosophical debate in the English-speaking world (and elsewhere) in the 1980s and 1990s largely took the form of a debate between "liberals" and "communitarians". The "liberals" in this debate defended Rawls's notion of a choosing subject made "thin" almost to the point of insubstantiality by a "thick" veil of ignorance about his own traits and qualities. The "communitarians" argued that validly choosing subjects had necessarily to remain "thick" subjects with conscious commitments to the values and beliefs of the "communities" that they belonged to. For the anti-Rawlsian position see, for example, Michael Sandel, Liberalism and the Limits of Justice, Cambridge University Press, 1981.

67 See John Harsanyi, Can the Maximin Principle Serve as a Base for Morality? A Critique of John Rawls's Theory in The American Political Science Review 69 pp. 594-606. Harsanyi uses the following example to argue that the maximin rule is difficult to apply to everyday life: if someone living in New York were considering which to choose of two jobs – a merely mediocre job in his home city and another, very good job in Chicago which would involve, however, his flying to this latter city in order to take it up – Rawls's "maximin principle" would dictate that this person would turn down the better job in Chicago already

just for the reason that the plane on which he would have to fly there might, on a "worst-case scenario", crash. This, argues Harsanyi, illustrates how inapplicable to real life Rawls's maximin rule actually is. Rawls, indeed, would likely deny the relevance of Harsanyi's example to his theory, arguing that, whereas what is evoked in this example is just a single temporary and limited risk (that involved in taking a plane for a single flight), the question decided on by the parties in the original position bears rather on structures in which these parties will live for their entire future lives.

68   John Rawls, A Theory of Justice (Revised Edition), Oxford University Press 1999, p. 118.
69   John Rawls, The Law of Peoples, Harvard University Press, Cambridge Massachusetts, 1999, p. 37
70   Ibid.
71   Ibid. p. 38.
72   John Rawls, A Theory of Justice (Revised Edition), Oxford University Press 1999, p. 68.
73   Ibid. p. 17.
74   Ibid.
75   Ibid. pp. 128-129.
76   Ibid. p. 46.
77   Ibid. p. 11.
78   See the critique developed by Michael Walzer in his book Interpretation and Social Criticism (Harvard University Press, Cambridge, Massachusetts, 1987, p. 20 ff.). Walzer critiques Rawls's whole conception as mere "constructivism", offering the following parody of this latter: people from various different countries come together in some neutral, history-less location – say, on the moon – and agree there on a consensual principle of justice. Their discussions with one another are conducted in Esperanto, since they are under a "veil of ignorance" and have all forgotten the countries they come from and the languages respectively spoken there. But why, asks Walzer, would any of these people, once they had returned to the places they came from, feel any obligation to abide by agreements struck on the moon? Rawls, it has to be said, might reply, in his own defence, simply as follows: "Because the agreements struck on the moon were just and fair".
79   John Rawls, A Theory of Justice (Revised Edition), Oxford University Press 1999, p. 68.

80   Ibid.
81   Ibid. p. 14.
82   Ibid. p. 8.

Already published in the same series:

Walther Ziegler
Camus in 60 Minutes
ISBN 9783741227738

Walther Ziegler
Freud in 60 Minutes
ISBN 9783741227707

Walther Ziegler
Hegel in 60 Minutes
ISBN 9783741227677

Walther Ziegler
Heidegger in 60 Minutes
ISBN 9783741227752

Walther Ziegler
Kant in 60 Minutes
ISBN 9783741226373

Walther Ziegler
Marx in 60 Minutes
ISBN 9783741227691

Walther Ziegler
Nietzsche in 60 Minutes
ISBN 9783752803822

Walther Ziegler
Platon in 60 Minutes
ISBN 9783741227615

Walther Ziegler
Sartre in 60 Minutes
ISBN 9783741227653

Walther Ziegler
Rousseau in 60 Minutes
ISBN 9783741227622

Walther Ziegler
Smith in 60 Minutes
ISBN 9783741227721

Walther Ziegler
Rawls in 60 Minutes
ISBN 9783750424050

Walther Ziegler
Wittgenstein in 60 Minutes

Walther Ziegler
Adorno in 60 Minutes

Walther Ziegler
Hobbes in 60 Minutes

Walther Ziegler
Popper in 60 Minutes

Coming soon in the same series:

Walther Ziegler
Arendt in 60 Minutes

Walther Ziegler
Foucault in 60 Minutes

Walther Ziegler
Habermas in 60 Minutes

Walther Ziegler
Schopenhauer in 60 Minutes

The author:

Dr Walther Ziegler is academically trained in the fields of philosophy, history and political science. As a foreign correspondent, reporter and newsroom coordinator for the German TV station ProSieben he has produced films on every continent. His news reports have won several prizes and awards.He has also authored numerous books in the field of philosophy. His many years of experience as a journalist mean that he is able to present the complex ideas of the great philosophers in a way that is both engaging and very clear. Since 2007 he has also been active as a teacher and trainer of young TV journalists in Munich, holding the post of Academic Director at the Media Academy, an institute of higher education that offers film and TV courses at its base directly on the site of the major European film production company Bavaria Film.